A Sky Full of Emotions

"There is a color for every feeling,
and it shines bright for all to see."

By: Skylar Crocker

Illustrated by: Stallion Studios 89

Editor: Kimberly Green

KG Writings

This book is dedicated to my mommy,
who has taught me about all my emotions and
how to handle them when I am alone.

I love you,

Skylar

This book is intended for promoting emotional intelligence in youth.

Teaching children about their feelings at an early age helps promote empathy, offering a deeper nurturing connection.

The goal is to help children identify their emotions and learn to process their feelings healthily. Ensuring they grow into emotionally healthy adults.

(As you read, look for **asterisks on the pages to promote dialogue.)

Hi, I'm Skylar, and I'm full of **emotions!**

What are **emotions?**

Emotions are the ways your body <u>feels</u> throughout your day.

They are a part of you and me.

We all have **emotions** but can <u>feel</u> and show them in different ways. I like to put colors to the **emotions** I <u>feel</u>. My <u>feelings</u> can shine blue like the ocean or yellow like the sun.

Come along with me as I show you my rainbow of **emotions!**

I wake up early with a big yawn and a stretch.
Then I get dressed, brush my teeth, and eat breakfast.

School days are the best, and I get soooooooo excited!
It's hard to stay still when you're <u>feeling</u> this way,
so I dance a little at the beginning of my day.

What **emotion** am I <u>feeling</u> in the morning?

EXCITED

**What does exciting <u>feel</u> like to you?

At school, we learn about all kinds of things. Writing, spelling, and math are a few. My favorite lesson is math. The numbers are fun to count. Look at the 100% at the top of my test!

My smile was so big because I was _feeling_ so *proud*!

What is the **emotion** I _feel_?

PROUD

**What things have you done that make you _feel_ proud?

At recess, my best friend is not here to play with me. I _feel_ very sad, so sad that my eyes fill up with tears. Another classmate asked me to come to play with her to try and cheer me up.

What is the **emotion** I _feel_?

SAD

**What can you do when you see someone sad?

It's time for show and tell in class. I brought my stuffed animal I sleep with every night, but I am a little *nervous* about sharing it. My stomach starts to <u>feel</u> funny, like a bunch of butterflies are flying inside my tummy.

When I show the class my unicorn, they smile and clap!

What is the **emotion** I <u>feel</u>?

NERVOUS

**How do you <u>feel</u> the emotion nervous?
Do you ever <u>feel</u> like butterflies are in your tummy?

At lunch, I opened my lunchbox to my *surprise!*

My mom had packed my favorites; sushi, grapes, strawberry muffin, and apple juice.

YUMMY, the best!

What is the **emotion** I <u>feel</u>?

SURPRISED

**What kind of surprises do you like?

After all of our lessons, we play a dancing game.
We get to be as *silly* as we want, and it is a great ending to the school day!

What is the **emotion** I <u>feel</u>?

SILLY

**What is something silly you like to do?

At home, I get to play with my brothers. We have so much fun until Mom says, "Time to get ready for bed." I get so *angry* because I do not want the day to end.

I huff and puff and stomp off to my room.

What is the **emotion** I <u>feel</u>?

ANGRY

**What helps calm you down when you are angry?

Mom says, "Sky Pie, you know how the rain pours, how it thunders and lightenings in those scary storms. Shortly after the rain stops, a giant rainbow appears. It is beautiful and radiant with all of its colors. You must rest your storm of emotions; you have let it rain, and when you wake up, you will shine again. You're my sky full of emotions. Your rainbow of emotions is beautiful."

Now I can sleep _feeling_ loved.

What is the **emotion** I _feel_?

LOVED

**What makes you _feel_ loved?

My **emotions** are a part of me.

I can <u>feel</u> them and express them.

It's good to know how you <u>feel</u> and to be mindful
of how others <u>feel</u> around you.

Colorful **emotions** fill up our day!

Write about your **emotions** and what
they <u>feel</u> like to you.

Draw the colors you <u>feel</u> with each **emotion**.

Remember what made you <u>feel</u> that way.

Remember how that <u>feeling</u> felt in your body.

My Emotions Diary

*** If you have multiple children, use index cards to do this exercise—one side to write and the other side to draw a picture

What are some emotions you felt today?

Draw a picture of your emotions.

What are some emotions you felt today?

_____

_____

_____

_____

_____

_____

_____

_____

_____

_____

_____

_____

_____

Draw a picture of your emotions.

What are some emotions you felt today?

_____

- -

- -

- -

- -

- -

- -

- -

- -

- -

- -

- -

- -

Draw a picture of your emotions.

What are some emotions you felt today?

_____

_____

_____

_____

_____

_____

_____

_____

_____

_____

_____

_____

Draw a picture of your emotions.

What are some emotions you felt today?

_____

_____

_____

_____

_____

_____

_____

_____

_____

_____

_____

_____

_____

Draw a picture of your emotions.

What are some emotions you felt today?

_____

_____

_____

_____

_____

_____

_____

_____

_____

_____

_____

_____

_____

Draw a picture of your emotions.

What are some emotions you felt today?

_____

_____

_____

_____

_____

_____

_____

_____

_____

_____

_____

_____

_____

Draw a picture of your emotions.

What are some emotions you felt today?

_____

_____

_____

_____

_____

_____

_____

_____

_____

_____

_____

_____